C0-AKF-424

# Inchies

Create miniature works of art using textiles
and mixed media techniques

Edited by Peggy Donda-Kobert

# Inchies

## Create miniature works of art using textiles and mixed media techniques

Search Press

# contents

# Working with different materials

## Materials

# Authors

## Peggy Donda-Kobert

Even as a child, I was fascinated by fabrics. My granny, who was a dressmaker and haberdasher, inspired me to start collecting little pieces of fabric. At first, I used to make new clothes for my doll; later I designed my own clothing. In 2002, I started doing traditional patchwork. Later on, I discovered art quilts and loved them, as they made use of lots of materials that did not appear to be related to textiles. This was what led me to experiment. Since then, I have enjoyed working with smaller items, such as ATCs (Artist Trading Cards) and AMCs (Artist Mailing Cards). Creativa, in Dortmund, invited me to run workshops on the subject of inchies. At the same time, I set up an Internet group, which continues to attract new members. I talk about my work at:
http://create-fabric-art-doko.blogspot.com.

## Momo Jacob

My real name is Monika Jacob, but in the realm of textiles I am known as Momo. I live with my husband and two foster children in a pretty, half-timbered house in southern Lower Saxony, and I work as a teacher.
Since 2003, I have been working with fabrics, starting with traditional patchwork by hand and machine, then 'Crazy' patchwork and then on to modern dressmaking and sewing techniques. I particularly like to experiment with creative materials and work with old, recycled materials and things that I have to hand. This was also what originally aroused my interest in quilts, and so I came full circle back to traditional patchwork.
In recent years, I have participated in various shows, including those at Nordheim, Munich and Einbeck (on the patchwork days). I talk about my 'sewing experiments' at:
http://nadelprobe.blogspot.com.

## Waltraud Riegler-Baier

I live with my family on the edge of the Swabian Mountains. I work as a teacher in a secondary school. One of the subjects I teach is textiles and handicrafts. In 2003, I took a patchwork course and rediscovered my love of fabrics. Two trips to the USA reinforced my enthusiasm for textile materials.
Initially, I focused more on traditional patchwork, especially as I found interesting blogs on the Internet on the subject of freehand textile techniques. Felting using an embellisher and hand embroidery particularly appealed to me. I was able to get new ideas and learn new techniques from courses with many renowned lecturers. You can see my work at:
http://farbtupfer.blogspot.com.

## Ulla Stewart

I was brought up in the velvet and silk town of Krefeld. Both my parents worked in the textile industry and so I discovered my love of fabrics and colours early on. I started training to become a management assistant before I got married and had children.
When the children were older, I took over the management of a little workshop in Krefeld. Later, I managed the cutting department and workshop for a Dutch furniture company.
In 1980, I saw a quilt for the first time in my life at the Cologne furniture show, and, from that moment on, I knew that that was what I wanted to make. In Germany, the quilting scene was very small, so I turned to the Netherlands. My first quilts were exhibited in smaller shows, along with those of other like-minded people. At the same time, I taught on courses and in workshops. Over time, my quilts became smaller and smaller. I got to know other textile designers via the Internet and swapped ideas with them. Using these new techniques and materials, I began to make AMCs and then ATCs. Now, I love producing inchies and working creatively with them. Take a look at my blog at:
http://ullas-art.blogspot.com.

# Foreword

by Peggy Donda-Kobert

This book is intended for all those who enjoy working with textiles and who want to try out new techniques and materials.

Inchies are works of art in miniature format, exactly 1 x 1in square, or 2.5 x 2.5cm. This is what makes working with them so exciting. Their tiny size makes them perfect for experimenting. Impressive inchies can be made with minimal quantities of materials, a lot of which can be found in nature, in the kitchen or in your workbox.

In this book, various authors present techniques they hope will excite and inspire you. Experiment with them, and play with the various materials, to your heart's content.

The projects described show a number of ways in which inchies can be used as decoration, thus giving them an additional practical use. Inchies that you are collecting for future use can be kept in coin-collecting pockets, arranged according to colour and theme.

Take a look at the Internet, where you will find even more great ideas on the subject of inchies.

Now, just go and have fun with this book!

Regards,

# Producing inchies

by Peggy Donda-Kobert

Inchies are little works of art in miniature format, 1 × 1in (2.5 × 2.5cm) in size. They can be made from many different materials, such as fabric, paper, metal, felt or similar. Inchies get their unmistakable character from the materials used.

To give textile materials, such as fabric or felt, the required stability, the reverse of the inchie is reinforced. As well as simple card or stiff fabric, stabiliser is particularly good here, and is available from retailers in various strengths. Stabilisers such as S 320 or S 520 by Freudenberg can be ironed on permanently. Pelmet Vilene or S 80, also by Freudenberg, can be attached using textile adhesive. Double-sided adhesive stabiliser (e.g. Vliesofix by Freudenberg) is applied to the reverse side.
Using a stabiliser is very important when you need to neaten the edge of the inchie using a sewing machine. It will prevent the small pieces from slipping under the sewing-machine foot.

Cut out 2.5 × 2.5cm (1 × 1in) pieces of the stabiliser and then fix them to the reverse of the fabric. Or, alternatively, cut out generously sized pieces of the fabric and stabiliser, fix them together, and then cut into 2.5cm (1in) squares.

When making an inchie, the order of work is important and will depend upon the accessories used. If you are attaching things such as buttons, stones, beads, etc., the inchie should be neatened first by machine, as the sewing-machine foot will not be able to glide over the raised materials at a later stage. An alternative would be to neaten the edge of the inchie by hand afterwards.

The outside edges can be neatened using a narrow zigzag stitch or a satin stitch. For a clean edge, the needle should fall outside the inchie to the right and into the fabric to the left. A straight stitch 1–2mm (approx. ⅛in) away from the edge also works well and is sufficient to permanently join the surface to the backing. Many sewing machines have numerous decorative stitches that can also be used.
If you want to sew your inchies by hand, the edge can be neatened with buttonhole stitch or blanket stitch.
For fabrics that are joined using adhesive stabiliser, you probably will not need to neaten the edges, as they are unlikely to fray.

Various accessories can be attached to the surface of your inchie. A wide range of materials can be used, depending on the theme. Small buttons, various beads and colourful sequins can be applied in different ways. Lace and old braid trimming add a nostalgic touch. Natural materials, such as little shells, pieces of wood or bits of metal, create an attractive finish. Stamps or parts of photographs add an artistic touch. Most of these decorations can be attached using a sewing machine. Others are better sewn on by hand with a few stitches. Fabric adhesive or a hot-glue gun can also be used for fixing.

## Swapping inchies

A few words on the subject of swapping: for some time, there have been numerous groups on the Internet that take on joint projects and swap the results. It is not just about swapping finished inchies either; you can also swap fabrics, beads, yarns and ribbons, thus increasing the range of materials available to you. Ideas are exchanged too, creating a rich pool of inspiration, and you will be amazed by just how imaginative and creative your fellow participants can be!

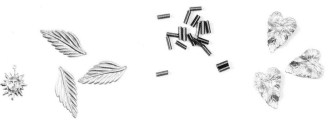

# Completely natural

by Peggy Donda-Kobert

You can always draw inspiration from the colours and shapes in nature. From spring through to late autumn little things, such as flowers, leaves or fruits, can be collected. Little shells or pieces of bark, twigs, feathers or tiny stones can be used as well. Retailers also offer many natural materials for use in craftwork, such as tiny pieces of coconut or buttons made from wood, mother-of-pearl or bone. The predominant colours are in the beige to brown range. Using various fabrics, such as jute, linen, silk or felt, can add even more interest to the completed picture.

## Materials

- various neutral-coloured fabrics
- threads in beige through to brown
- wooden buttons, wooden beads, etc.
- craft glue

## TIP
You can also use spices from the kitchen, such as cloves, star anise or coffee beans, to make great decorations for your inchies.

## Instructions

### 1. Consider:
Where to place the inchies you are using for this theme. If your creation is to be placed beneath an old window frame, without the glass, you can use raised pieces such as buttons, beads and little pieces of wood or stones. If the inchies are going to lie under glass, then you need to take into consideration the distance between them and the glass.

### 2. Consider:
What materials you will be using on the surface. All inchies on to which pictures, lace, feathers or other flat pieces will be placed can be neatened by machine after decorating. If you are using buttons, twigs or similar things, neaten the inchie first and then sew or glue on the items.

Use a hot-glue gun to stick on larger and heavier pieces, such as little stones or cinnamon sticks. This practical tool can be used to fix the desired pieces permanently on to the inchie.

Smaller pieces, such as bits of shell, tiny buttons or beads, can look a bit lonely, even on such a small piece as an inchie. To avoid this, simply place a piece of lace, organza or jute underneath them and attach it at the same time.

Very white fabric or lace should be dyed, otherwise it will stand out too much, spoiling the natural look of the project. You can use strong coffee or tea for this. Leave the fabric or lace for a while, soaking in the liquid, and then leave it to dry without rinsing out.

The decorative pieces on the inchie do not have to finish exactly at the edge. If feathers, lace or raffia overhang slightly, the whole image will look more natural.

11

# WORKING WITH THEMES

# Seasons

by Peggy Donda-Kobert

Each season has its own characteristics, which can be symbolised by a different colour. Winter is icy and white; spring is characterised by its delicate, bright flowers and leaves; summer is bright and cheerful and autumn is known for the colourful, warm colours of the falling leaves. The seasons are an ideal subject for inchies.

The following project was the joint work of four people. The inchies were worked on for a whole year and then exchanged and grouped into their relevant seasons. The advantage of the exchange is obvious: not only could four times the number of similar materials be used, but the number of ideas was quadrupled too.

## Instructions

By working in sets, several inchies can be made at the same time. To make four inchies, cut out squares measuring 10 × 10cm (4 × 4in) from a suitable fabric, as well as from the iron-on stabiliser that you intend to use. Iron the stabiliser on to the reverse of the fabric and cut into four inchies. Place Pelmet Vilene underneath and neaten the outside edges using the sewing machine. Finally, sew on the accessories by hand or by machine.

Seasonal Swap
2009

Peggy Donda-Kobert

create-fabric-art-doko.blogspot.com

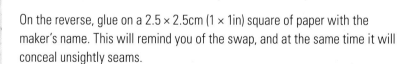

On the reverse, glue on a 2.5 × 2.5cm (1 × 1in) square of paper with the maker's name. This will remind you of the swap, and at the same time it will conceal unsightly seams.

## Materials

- various remnants of fabric, in colours corresponding to the seasons
- iron-on stabiliser, e.g. S 320 by Freudenberg
- stiff stabiliser, e.g. Pelmet Vilene
- accessories, e.g. snowflakes, flowers, shells and leaves

## Spring inchie

### Materials:
- various bits of yarn in green and pink
- monofilament (transparent thread) for the machine
- decorative spring flower
- small yellow bead
- iron-on stabiliser, e.g. S 320 by Freudenberg

### Instructions:

Place small, cut-up bits of yarn in a dense layer on to a piece of baking parchment, so that there are no gaps in-between. Cut the stabiliser a little larger than needed for the inchies. Place the side with the iron-on coating downwards on to the bits of yarn and iron on. Set up the sewing machine for freehand embroidery and lower the feed dog.
The stitching should simply fix the yarns and be barely visible. For this, use transparent thread for the upper thread. Turn the stabiliser over and iron on the reverse, which will help to fix the yarns placed on the front.
Cut out the individual inchies and snip off any excess yarn with scissors. Sew on the flower by hand and place a little yellow bead in the centre. Leave the edge of the inchie raw.

## Summer inchie

### Materials:
- bits of wool and embroidery yarn in shades of beige and blue
- monofilament (transparent thread) for the machine
- shells, tiny starfish, etc.
- craft glue
- stiff stabiliser, e.g. S 80 by Freudenberg or Pelmet Vilene

### Instructions:

Cut out the stabiliser a little larger than an inchie.
Draw two lines on it 2.5cm (1in) apart (the various yarns will be sewn between these).
Sort the various bits of wool and embroidery yarn according to colour and place on to the inchie. Start at the bottom edge using the turquoise-coloured yarn. As you move up the inchie, use progressively lighter shades of blue and finish with white about one-third from the top.
Complete the remaining third with beige yarns to represent the sand.
Thread the top of the sewing machine with the monofilament and stitch over the bits of wool and embroidery yarn. The transparent thread will fix the yarn beneath it almost invisibly. Attach shells or little starfish using craft glue.

## Autumn inchie

### Materials:

- grey fabric for the background
- grey pen
- three different multicoloured yarns
- silver metallic and grey thread
- stiff stabiliser, e.g. S 80 by Freudenberg or Pelmet Vilene
- double-sided adhesive stabiliser (e.g. Vliesofix by Freudenberg)

### Instructions:

Iron the grey fabric on to the stabiliser using double-sided adhesive stabiliser. With a grey pen, draw on the outline of an umbrella. Lower the feed dog on the sewing machine and set up the machine for freehand embroidery. Embroider each of the three areas between the spokes with a different multicoloured yarn.
Embroider over the umbrella by hand using knot stitch in silver yarn, to give the impression of raindrops. Neaten the outside edges of the inchie with grey thread.

## Winter inchie

### Materials:

- dark blue fabric for the background
- Angelina fibres, fabric Tyvek
- silver stars and beads
- stiff stabiliser, e.g. S 80 by Freudenberg or Pelmet Vilene
- thread for neatening

### Instructions:

Place a thin layer of Angelina fibres on to dark blue fabric that has been stiffened with stabiliser. Make sure the fabric is still just visible. Fix the fibres between two layers of baking parchment using the iron. Start off at a low temperature. If the temperature is too high, the Angelina fibres can become matt. If the fibres are not melting properly, gradually increase the temperature.
To give the impression of the last remains of melting snow, melt a little piece of fabric Tyvek and stick it on using craft glue. Fabric Tyvek creates smaller bubbles than paper Tyvek. Once the outside edges have been neatened, stars and beads can be sewn on as desired.

# Christmas

by Peggy Donda-Kobert

How about little squares to decorate your Christmas tree? They are so quick to make that you could even start them during Advent. Christmas inchies look best in a 5 × 5cm (2 × 2in) size, so that they are clearly visible against the tree.

## Cut out

- 5 × 5cm (2 × 2in) Christmas fabrics
- 5 × 5cm (2 × 2in) Fast2Fuse

## Instructions

Fast2Fuse is a double-sided iron-on stabiliser that also has a little volume, giving the inchies a bit more fullness on the tree.
Place the fabric on to the stabiliser and fix with the iron – this should take about 10 seconds. Turn the inchie over and place a thin piece of cord folded into a loop about 10cm (4in) long on to the Fast2Fuse. Place the second piece of fabric on top and fix all the layers with the iron.

Neaten the edges with a matching gold or silver thread. Sew on little bells, beads, ribbons or stars to decorate.

## Materials

- various Christmas fabrics
- gold or silver metallic thread
- little bells, beads, ribbons and stars
- stiff stabiliser with iron-on coating on both sides, e.g. Fast2Fuse
- thin cord in gold or silver
- baking parchment

## TIP
Place the fabric and the Fast2Fuse together between two layers of baking parchment for iron fixing. The iron will then not stick to the stabiliser.

# From tulle to turquoise

by Ulla Stewart

Everyone has a favourite colour, and they probably have quite a lot of materials in shades of this colour in their collection, including fabrics, yarns lace, buttons, beads, sequins and bits of wool.

Depending on the materials used and how they are combined, your favourite colour will be featured in varying shades in this piece: from light to dark, intense to pale, bright to muted. Viewed as a whole, however, the basic colour will be the same, giving it a uniform appearance. The combination of different shades makes for an interesting design, and a variety of effects is possible.

## Materials

- fabric remnants
- buttons
- various yarns and fibres, e.g. Angelina
- bits of lace, beads, sequins and other embellishments

## Instructions

Working with just one colour is relatively easy. In order to create an interesting overall impression, black and white can also be used in very small quantities, as well as the adjacent colours on the colour wheel. For the colour turquoise, the neighbouring colour is green, and for red it is orange, for example. It is worth experimenting a little with colour to see the effects you can achieve.

Cut out the inchie in the basic colour and sew. Even a simple, basic fabric can be enhanced with Angelina fibres. Place various embellishments loosely on top and move them around until you are pleased with the arrangement. Look at your work from a distance, as this can help you achieve harmony between the colours selected. Once you are satisfied, sew on the individual elements and decorate further with beads and sequins, as desired.

# Bracelet in blue & orange

by Peggy Donda-Kobert

Even these tiny little pieces of fabric can be used effectively; colourful, interesting and varied in size, like slices of pizza, they can be rearranged however you wish. The pizza technique works well with the tiniest scraps of fabric fixed to a background and then decorated with yarn. As well as multicoloured yarns, special-effect and metallic threads can be used to form an interesting and varied surface.

For these inchies, just two colours were used (blue and orange), showing that even this is enough to achieve an exciting effect with such a multifaceted technique.

## Materials

- fabric in two different colours
- stiff, double-sided iron-on stabiliser, e.g. Fast2Fuse
- various special-effect yarns
- thin wire and beads
- jewellery clasp to secure the bracelet

## Instructions

Cut the fabrics into little pieces using a cutting wheel or scissors. Cut out a strip of Fast2Fuse, as well as a strip of fabric for the reverse of the bracelet that is long enough to go round your wrist and 2.5cm (1in) wide. Place the fabric for the reverse on to the Fast2Fuse and iron on between two layers of baking parchment. Turn over and arrange the tiny scraps of fabric on to the other side of the Fast2Fuse.

The fabric pieces can overlap the edge, as it will be cut off later. Make sure, though, that no white Fast2Fuse edges can be seen.

Iron the individual layers together once more between baking parchment.
Neaten off any uneven edges with scissors or a cutting wheel and then cut the
strip into inchies.
Use a decorative stitch around the raw fabric edges or oversew with special-effect
yarns. When you have neatened the outside edges of the inchies, attach the
individual inchies to each other using thin wire, placing a bead between each
square. Form a bracelet and sew on a clasp to secure.

# Beneath the rainbow

by Ulla Stewart

These little cubes are a very unusual gift idea. In their rainbow colours, they would make great boxes for a chocolate or even for a folded banknote. Even though they are admittedly a bit fiddly to make, they are definitely worth the effort.

## Materials
- various fabric remnants
- matching decorative pieces
- ribbon
- stiff stabiliser, e.g. S 80 by Freudenberg

## Instructions

To make a cube, you need six inchies in the same colour. Neaten the edges with a matching thread.

Lay out the six inchies face down as shown above and sew them together using a simple zigzag stitch.

Fold up the four side pieces and sew the sides of the cube together by hand, one after the other. It is best to use a simple zigzag stitch for this.

Close the lid that was sewn on in the first step.
Sew a ribbon loop to one of the sides to fasten the cube.
Decorate the individual surfaces of the cube, apart from the base on which
it will stand. Attach an extra-large bead or a button to the top with which
to fasten the cube.

# Neutral-coloured boxes

by Ulla Stewart

Homemade inchies are ideal for decorating small gifts. Here they are used as an interesting and varied decoration on a small box, providing a finishing touch for a special gift. Neutral colours decorated with matching lace and braid give these boxes a particularly elegant appearance.

## Materials

- neutral fabrics and lace
- matching silk thread
- very stiff, double-sided, iron-on stabiliser, e.g. S 133 by Freudenberg
- thin, double-sided, iron-on, volume stabiliser, e.g. H 630 by Freudenberg
- matching neutral materials for decoration, e.g. lace or braid
- craft glue

### Cut out for bottom and lid:

- two 7.5 × 7.5cm (3 × 3in) fabric squares for the outside
- two 7.5 × 7.5cm (3 × 3in) fabric squares for the inside
- two 7.5 × 7.5cm (3 × 3in) pieces of stiff stabiliser (e.g. S 133)
- 7.5 × 7.5cm (3 × 3in) piece of volume stabiliser (e.g. H 630) for the lid

### Cut out for the side pieces:

- four 5 × 7.5cm (2 × 3in) pieces of fabric for the outside
- four 5 × 7.5cm (2 × 3in) pieces of fabric for the inside
- four 5 × 7.5cm (2 × 3in) pieces of stiff stabiliser (e.g. S 133)

## Instructions

For each side of the box, iron on to one side of each piece of stiff stabiliser the fabric for the outside, and on to the other side the fabric for the inside. For the lid only, iron the volume stabiliser in-between the outside fabric and the stiff stabiliser to achieve greater volume. Neaten all the edges with matching thread. Decorate the lid and the outside pieces with lace and braid however you wish.

Lay out the squares and the four rectangles face down to form the box (see also page 22). Sew the individual pieces together using a wide zigzag stitch and matching thread. Join up the side edges by hand.

Make inchies for the lid and side pieces and glue them on using craft glue. Inchies made from the same fabric as the box look very pretty. Decorate the inchies with buttons, beads or sequins.

# Making fabrics rusty

by Peggy Donda-Kobert

Making fabric rusty is fascinating work. You can achieve great effects with this unusual dyeing technique. Use nails, horseshoes, washers and similar items made from metals that rust. Interesting shapes are formed on the fabric, depending on the objects used.

## Materials

- an old, flat container
- various light fabrics, lace, etc.
- vinegar
- nails, washers and other metal objects that rust
- spunbond fibres, Tyvek, beads
- multicoloured yarns

### TIP
Galvanised nails or other treated metals are not suitable as they do not rust.

## Instructions

Wet the fabric and lay it in a flat container. Place a layer of nails or similar on top and then a layer of fabric on top of that. The fabric can be creased or folded. Fill up the container with a mixture of water and a large dash of vinegar until all of the fabric is covered. Do not use an air-tight cover for the tin, as oxygen is necessary for the rusting process. Patience is now required, as fabrics react differently to the rusting process. We recommend that you check daily to see how far the rusting has progressed. When you are pleased with the effect achived, wash the finished fabric out well under warm running water and leave to dry.

When selecting which bits of the fabric to use, this little aid can be useful. Cut out a square of dark card measuring 10 × 10cm (4 × 4in) and cut out a 2.5 × 2.5cm (1 × 1in) square from the middle. By using this little frame, you can find the best places for cutting out an inchie, without being distracted by the rest of the piece of fabric.

When sewing rusty fabrics, watch out for tiny rust particles collecting in the fabric itself, making the fabric rough. To avoid tearing the weave, sew very slowly by machine. The inchies can be decorated with various accessories, including painted and melted-on Tyvek, painted spunbond fibres, etc.
Similar effects to rusting can be achieved with steam-fixed silk paints. Wet the fabric and lay it, creased, in a microwaveable dish. Sprinkle over the colour until the whole fabric is soaked in colour. Put in the microwave for approx. two minutes and heat. The result is similar to that obtained by rusting.

# Angelina fibres

by Peggy Donda-Kobert and Ulla Stewart

Angelina is an artificial fibre, available in heat-bondable and non-heat-bondable forms. Both types are available in many different colours that can be mixed to make new, varied colours.

The fibres are melted together between two layers of baking parchment using an iron. Start off using low temperatures. If the temperature is too hot or the iron remains on the fibres for too long, the colours can change or even become dull.

When bonding Angelina fibre make sure that you are working in a well-ventilated room.

## Materials

- bondable Angelina fibres in silver
- beads, gemstones, tulle, etc.
- baking parchment
- stiff stabiliser, e.g. Pelmet Vilene
- matching thread

## Instructions

Lay a sufficient quantity of Angelina fibres between two layers of baking parchment and bond briefly. The bonded Angelina should be slightly larger than that needed for the number of inchies to be made from it.

Once the baking parchment has cooled, cut the Angelina piece into two strips measuring 7.5 × 2.5cm (3 × 1in). Lay a piece of Pelmet Vilene of the same size between the two pieces of Angelina and neaten the edges with a narrow satin stitch. After cutting up the strip into inchies, neaten the remaining edges in the same way.

If the inchies are to be used as pendants, attach an eyelet to the corner of each one. A chain can then be attached later. Eyelets are tiny rings that are secured with a special tool called a setter.

The inchies can be decorated however you wish, using beads, sequins, tulle or matching buttons. Inchies look very elegant made using gold Angelina fibres and decorated with matching accessories.

# WORKING WITH DIFFERENT MATERIALS

# Tyvek

by Peggy Donda-Kobert

Fabric Tyvek has many uses in industry, for example as packaging material, and as protective clothing for those working in space technology, operating theatres and forensic laboratories.

Tyvek is available in fabric and paper form, both of which can be used to create wonderful effects in the field of art and craft. It begins to crumple at a temperature of approx. 118°C and at 135°C it starts to melt. Tyvek, in its smooth state, can be stitched using a sewing machine. Tyvek can be heated to give a three-dimensional effect. A breathing mask must be used for this. Parts of the Tyvek can be melted using a soldering iron. Larger areas can be melted using a hot-air dryer or an iron. You need to work carefully, for if too high a temperature is reached, all the Tyvek will quickly disappear.

## Instructions

Paint on both sides of a sufficiently large piece of Tyvek. This will prevent unsightly white spots appearing on the surface after melting. Liquid fabric paint is the best to use. Lay the Tyvek between two layers of baking parchment and hover the iron over the top. The Tyvek will change shape very quickly and shrink together, with bubbles appearing on the underside. With further heating, or when the iron is placed briefly on the baking parchment, the Tyvek will begin to dissolve. This will also form interesting textures.

## Materials
- Tyvek
- fabric paint or acrylic paint
- magnetic strip
- craft glue

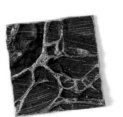

When cool, cut out inchies from the Tyvek and stick the underside, where
the bubbles are, on to a piece of the magnetic strip.
The creases in the Tyvek and the edges can be additionally emphasised
with gold paint. Apply the colour using a sponge.

# Inchies using various yarns

by Peggy Donda-Kobert

You do not always have to use ready-made fabric – you can also make interesting surfaces yourself. Various special-effect yarns can be used for this, and combined with tiny pieces of fabric, dyed muslin or pieces of lace.

## Materials

- felt or fabric as a base
- various coloured yarns
- metallic threads
- water-soluble stabiliser
- single-sided iron-on stabiliser, e.g. S 320 by Freudenberg

> ### TIP
> When using felt, use a stabiliser that will dissolve in cold water, otherwise the felt will shrink.

## Instructions

Cut out a piece of felt or fabric; it should be a little larger than the number of inchies you want to make from it. Lay the various coloured yarns on top; cover with a layer of water-soluble stabiliser and pin. Water-soluble stabiliser is transparent and enables you to see your work, e.g. where the seams are.

Set the presser foot tension on the sewing machine to zero and lower the feed dog. Sew some lines over the piece of fabric using a freehand straight stitch, so that all the yarns are secured.

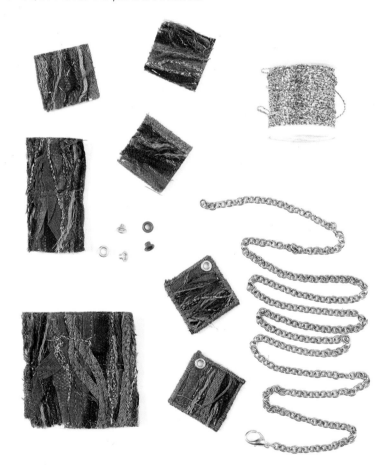

You can use coloured or metallic yarns and threads to make special accents. It is, however, recommended that you use transparent thread to secure the yarns initially, so that only the decorative threads are visible at the end. Rinse out the finished material thoroughly in water until you cannot feel any sticky stabiliser residue left.

When dry, iron the material on to the iron-on stabiliser (e.g. S 320). Cut out little squares measuring 2.5 × 2.5cm (1 × 1in) from it.
Neaten the outside edges with the sewing machine and further embellish the inchies as you wish.

# Felted inchies

by Waltraud Riegler-Baier

For some time now, felting has become increasingly significant in the area of textiles, as fabrics such as silk, organza or wool can all be felted. In addition to finished felt stabiliser, such as craft stabiliser, which is available in many colours, all sorts of other fabrics are also suitable for this process.

Small areas can be felted by hand. For larger areas, it is worth getting an embellisher. This special felting machine has up to twelve felting needles and can felt the fabric beneath them at high speed.

## Materials

- felting needles or embellisher
- craft felt
- fairy wool
- special-effect yarns
- organza
- embroidery yarn
- stiff stabiliser, e.g. S 80 by Freudenberg or Pelmet Vilene
- Styropor block

### TIP
Ironing on adhesive stabiliser is not recommended, as not only can the felt quickly turn 'flat', but it can also melt.

## Instructions

Lay a piece of craft felt on to a Styropor block. Place the various materials, such as fairy wool, special-effect yarns and organza on top, and felt together using felting needles. If the resulting surface is not to your liking, a new layer can be laid on top at any time.

What is different about felting needles are the little barbs that perform the felting process. The Styropor block underneath protects the needles. Felting by hand will take some time, as only one needle can be placed in the felt at a time. However, hand-felting needles are now available in a holder containing several needles, making it considerably faster to work.

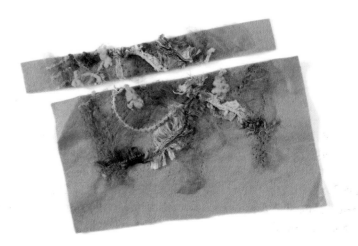

To make the felt inchies, felt a large area and then cut it into 2.5cm (1in) squares. Use Pelmet Vilene or S 80 to stabilise the felted inchies. Both types of stabiliser can easily be sewn by hand.
Sewing around the inchies by hand using blanket stitch emphasises the soft nature of the felt. The finished surface can be further decorated with beads or sequins as you wish.

# Inchies from silk

by Momo Jacob

Silk is still seen as an attractive textile material. Its sheen and texture have delighted people for thousands of years and it continues to inspire creativity today. As well as industrially dyed silk, self-dyed silk offers countless possibilities for creating decorative inchies. When combined with other materials, such as beads and sequins, there is no limit to its potential.

## Materials

- Pongé silk, approx. 50 × 50cm (20 × 20in)
- silk paints (steam-fix or iron-fix)
- double-sided adhesive stabiliser (e.g. Vliesofix by Freudenberg), approx. 30 × 30cm (12 × 12in)
- thin cotton fabric as a base, approx. 30 × 30cm (12 × 12in)
- felt as a base for the inchies 2.5 × 2.5cm (1 × 1in)
- embroidery or quilting yarns
- beads and small sequins
- single-sided, iron-on stabiliser, e.g. S 320 by Freudenberg

### TIP
Old silk painting cloths or silk remnants from other projects can be used for this technique.

## Instructions

Dye and fix the Pongé silk using the silk paint, according to the manufacturer's instructions.

Spread out some baking parchment over the ironing board as an undersheet. Lay out the double-sided adhesive stabiliser, remove the backing paper from the uppermost surface and drape the silk over it in folds, in any way you wish. Cover with another sheet of baking parchment to protect the iron and iron the folds on to the stabiliser. Cut off the excess silk around the stabiliser.

Remove the backing paper from the other side of the stabiliser and place it on to the pre-prepared cotton fabric. Iron again to fix the folded silk to the fabric beneath it.

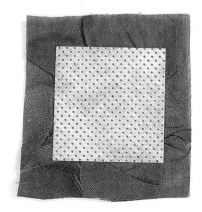

Cut out some pieces measuring
4 × 4cm (1.5 × 1.5in) from the silk.
Make sure that the more interesting
folds of silk are in the middle of the
squares as much as possible. Cut up
the single-sided stabiliser (e.g. S 320)
into 2.5 × 2.5cm (1 × 1in) squares and
place in the centre of the reverse of
the silk fabric. Iron it on.

Embroider the inchies with the various
yarns. As well as different machine
stitches, you can also sew decorative
stitches by hand. Perhaps turn over
a fold and emphasise it with a distinct
embroidery stitch. Finally, sew on
beads and small sequins.

Turn under a ½cm (¼in) seam
allowance all around the outside edge
and sew the silk to the cut-out felt
square. The seam can be sewn
invisibly or decoratively using
buttonhole stitch or oversewing.

# Fabric paper

by Peggy Donda-Kobert

Making fabric paper is easy and inexpensive. Its leather-like texture opens up new design opportunities and possibilities for creative experimentation. Fabric paper can be sewn easily either by hand or by machine, and can be combined with many other materials.

## Materials

- tissue paper
- light, plain-coloured fabric, e.g. cotton or other loose-weave fabrics
- neoprene textile adhesive or bookbinding glue
- fabric paints
- pieces of lace, thick yarns
- plastic film, preferably textured, as a backing

### TIP
Do not use traditional craft glue, as this often becomes relatively hard after drying.

## Instructions

Light fabrics, such as cotton, are good as a backing for the fabric paper. When finished, the backing will not be visible.

Spread out the textured plastic film on to a base. Mix the textile adhesive with water in a ratio of 3:2 and spread some of it on to the film. Lay the fabric on top and coat it with textile adhesive. In order to achieve an unusual texture, pieces of lace or thick yarns can be placed on top.

Crumple up the tissue paper and pull it apart again slightly. Lay it over the wet surface, retaining these folds.

Spread textile adhesive one last time over everything, being careful to avoid air bubbles forming.

Paint the fabric paper however you wish, using the fabric paints. Once it has dried overnight, it can easily be pulled away from the film, cut into the desired size and worked on further to create inchies. These can then be used for other projects, as you wish.

# Inchies from silk paper

by Momo Jacob

Silk paper is made from individual silk fibres. Although it is called 'paper', it is more like a kind of fabric. The material can be worked in a three-dimensional way like paper, yet it has the sheen and texture of silk.

## Materials

- silk fibres
- PVA glue or textile medium
- roller
- tulle, two pieces approx. 50 × 50cm (20 × 20in)
- paintbrush
- silk paints
- plastic sheeting
- embroidery yarn
- metallic thread
- silk ribbons

## Instructions

Stir together PVA glue and water in a ratio of around 1:10. For a sheet of silk paper, you will need to thoroughly mix together around a walnut-sized amount of glue with around ten times as much water.

Spread out the plastic sheeting and lay a piece of tulle on top. Hold the silk fibres lightly between the thumb and first finger of each hand. Pull out the silk fibres and, with dry hands, lay them out on the tulle in a grid. Lay the first layer horizontally, the next vertically and the final layer horizontally again. Several thin layers will stick better than a single thick layer.

Cover the laid silk fibres with a second piece of tulle. Carefully apply the glue/water mixture and, using the roller, work it in thoroughly by rolling to and fro in all directions. Gradually increase the pressure and work in more and more liquid.

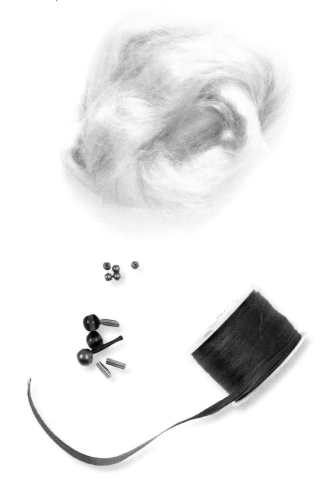

## TIP

As a precaution, rub handcream into your hands, so that the silk fibres do not catch on rough fingers.

When the first side is thoroughly soaked and rollered, turn the work over (the two pieces of tulle will continue to hold the silk fibres together) and proceed with the reverse side, using the roller again. Remove the tulle from the upper side. Carefully turn the silk paper over and remove the tulle from the other side too.

Apply the silk paints using a large paintbrush. On the wet background, the colours will run into one another like watercolours, forming new shades.

Leave the silk paper to dry on several layers of kitchen paper, preferably overnight. At this stage, folds can be made that will set during the drying process.

Cut the finished silk paper into squares measuring 2.5 × 2.5cm (1 × 1in) and decorate with the various yarns. Beads and sequins can also be sewn on. You can use the inchies for other projects in any way you wish, e.g. a hair slide (see above).

# Inchies with homemade beads

by Momo Jacob

Beads are available in numerous colours, shapes and sizes. With a little skill, you can make them yourself too. These beads are made from an unusual material – an orange net. Experiment, and try out different materials for making your beads.

## Instructions

Cut the orange net into strips approx. 1cm (½in) wide and 3–5cm (1¼–2in) long. Wind one of these strips several times around a knitting needle; catch one or two strips of tinsel at the same time and wind them in.
Lightly bond the netting using the hot-air gun; it will shrink together slightly and bond to the tinsel strips that have not melted.

## Materials

- felt as a base for the inchies
- orange or onion net
- strips of gold tinsel
- knitting needle
- hot-air gun or embossing heat gun
- matching thread

## TIP
Work in a well-ventilated room or outdoors.

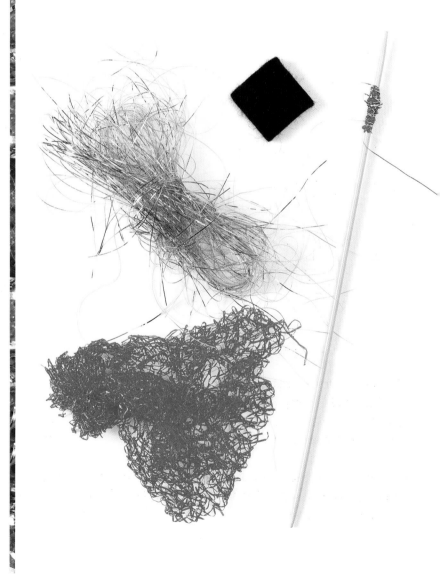

When heating, turn the knitting needle in your hand, so that the hot air touches the whole bead. You may need more or less time for the material to melt, depending on the temperature of the gun. After a brief cooling-down period, the bead can be slipped off the needle.

Sew the bead on to a felt inchie using matching thread. With small beads, several beads can be arranged on one inchie. The inchie can be used to make a brooch or other piece of jewellery.

# Creative variety

by Peggy Donda-Kobert

## Tools and accessories

It is definitely an advantage to be able to use a sewing machine when making inchies. All the inchies described in this book can, however, also be made by hand.

You will need an inch ruler to be able to cut out accurately. A cutting wheel and a cutting mat will make the cutting easier. An iron can be used not only for ironing, but also to distort heat-sensitive materials.

For some work, a hot-air gun is recommended. This can be used to melt a wide surface area. Even better is an embossing heat gun; it generates less airflow and is not quite as hot as a hot-air gun from DIY stores.

## Stabilisers

Many different stabilisers are available for stabilising fabric, and they are necessary for making inchies.

Pelmet Vilene or S 80 by Freudenberg is a stiffened stabiliser that is very good for writing on and painting, but is not designed to be an iron-on stabiliser.

S 320 and S 520 by Freudenberg have a permanent iron-on coating on one side, with S 520 being significantly more stable than S320. Both are very good for getting a better hold on the fabric when under the sewing-machine needle.

S 133 by Freudenberg is a very stable and compact interfacing with an iron-on coating on one side.

Ultra Stable by Gütermann Sulky is a stiffer embroidery stabiliser coated with an iron-on adhesive on one side.

Vliesofix, Steam-A-Seam or Bondaweb are thin adhesive stabilisers used to bind the base and the fabric. They are also very suitable for painting and appliqué work.

Fast2Fuse is a stiff, 2mm-thick interfacing with an iron-on coating on both sides.

Water-soluble stabiliser is available from various manufacturers under the names of Soluvlies, Avalon or Ultra Solvy.

## Creating surfaces

When making inchies, your remnants box will come into its own. Even the tiniest piece of fabric can be used. It does not matter what type of fabric is used either: denim, patchwork fabric, silk, jute or remnants of tulle, organza and felt can be used anywhere. To create the surface, wool, silk ribbon, special-effect yarns and many other materials are also suitable. Fabrics can be dyed with silk paints or painted with acrylic paints. Materials from the mixed-media field, such as Tyvek and Angelina, are also particularly good for creating texture.

You can use all kinds of beads, sequins, buttons, stamps and lace on the top of inchies. They can be embroidered, stuck, stamped or sewn on. Give your imagination free rein! Small pictures from magazines can serve to emphasise the theme, as well as letters, numbers or fragments of photographs.

To neaten the edges, normal sewing thread or embroidery yarn can be used. Special yarns can also give the inchie a lustrous finish. You can use machine-embroidery thread, metallic thread and bits of wool for this.

## Publication data

First published in Great Britain 2009 by Search Press
Limited, Wellwood, North Farm Road, Tunbridge Wells,
Kent TN2 3DR

Original Edition ©: 2009

World rights reserved by Christophorus Verlag GmbH,
Freiburg/Germany

Original German title: Inchies

English translation by Cicero Translations

English edition edited and typeset by GreenGate Publishing
Services, Tonbridge

All rights reserved. No part of this book, text, photographs
or illustrations may be reproduced or transmitted in any
form or by any means by print, photoprint, microfilm,
microfiche, photocopier, internet or in any way known or
as yet unknown, or stored in a retrieval system, without
written permission obtained beforehand from
Search Press.

Text: Peggy Donda-Kobert
Design and production: Peggy Donda-Kobert,
Momo Jacob, Waltraud Riegler-Bayer, Ulla Stewart
Editorial office (German edition): Christa Rolf
Editing (German edition): Angelika Klein
Photography: Uli Glasemann, Ulla Stewart (p. 28)
Jacket design (German edition): Aurélie Lambrecht
Layout and Production (German edition):
art und weise, Freiburg
Reproduction: Meyle & Müller, Pforzheim

ISBN 978-1-84448-483-6

Whilst the author and publisher have taken the greatest
care to ensure that all details and instructions are
correct, they cannot, however, be held responsible for any
consequences, whether direct or indirect, arising from
any errors.

# Manufacturers

Freudenberg KG, Vertrieb Vlieseline, Heidelberg
www.vlieseline.de

Gütermann AG, Gutach/Breisgau
www.guetermann.com

Madeira Garnfabrik Rudolf Schmidt KG, Freiburg
www.madeira.de

Prym-Consumer GmbH, Stolberg
www.prym-consumer.com

Rayher Hobbykunst, Laupheim
www.rayher-hobby.de

Union Knopf GmbH, Bielefeld
www.unionknopf.com

Hans Dill GmbH & Co KG, Bärnau
www.dill-buttons.de

Paints:

C.Kreul GmbH & Co. KG, Hallerndorf
www.c-kreul.de

Deka-Textilfarben, Unterhaching

Marabu GmbH & Co. KG, Tamm
www.marabu.de

Suppliers
For details of suppliers, please visit the Search Press
website:
www.searchpress.com

Although every attempt has been made to ensure that all
the materials and equipment used in this book are currently
available, the Publishers cannot guarantee that this will
always be the case. If you have difficulty in obtaining any
of the items mentioned, then suitable alternatives should
be used instead.

The authors would like to thank Susanne Neuhauser,
Barbara Hoppe, Kerstin Streich, Susanne Pflüger, Britta
Waag, Hannelore von der Heyde, Maria Garnitz and
Sigrid Artmeier for making their inchies available to
appear in this book.

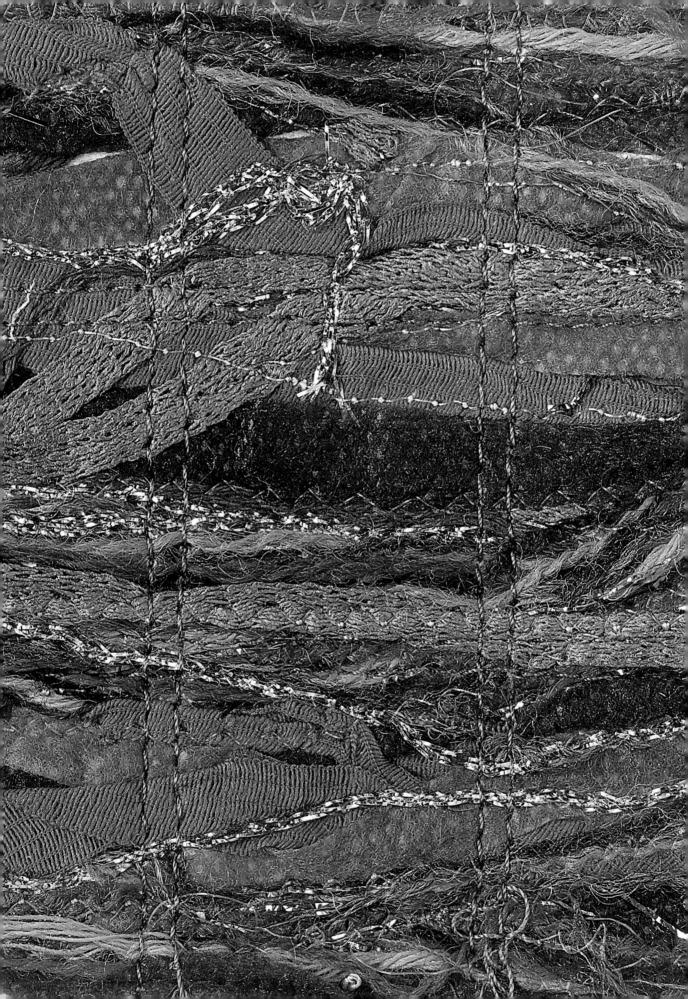